Moving to Britain from
Iraq

**Senker
Photography by Howard Davies**

W
FRANKLIN WATTS
LONDON · SYDNEY

First published in 2008 by Franklin Watts

Franklin Watts,
338 Euston Road,
London, NW1 3BH

Franklin Watts Australia,
Level 17/207 Kent Street,
Sydney, NSW 2000

Series editor: Sarah Peutrill
Art director: Jonathan Hair
Design: Rita Storey
Photographs: Howard Davies (unless otherwise stated)

The author and photographer would like to thank the following for
their help in the preparation of this book: the staff and children of
Adelaide Primary School, especially Neal McIlwaine and his class,
Deborah Taylor; Banoo, Bynar and Byshar Ali; Amena Haji Hassan;
Ali Omar; Jacob Whatmough-Stow; Jane Stow; Ruth Stow. We
would like to thank Banoo's family for permission to reproduce the
photos on cover inset and pages 12 ,13 (top) and 24 (bottom).

Picture credits: Marwan Ibrahim/AFP/Getty Images: 11.

Dewey number: 304.8'41'0567

ISBN: 978 0 7496 7856 2

Printed in China

Franklin Watts is a division of Hachette Children's Books,
an Hachette Livre UK company.

Contents

Words in **bold** are in the glossary on page 28.

All about me

My name is Banoo Ali and I am nine years old. My family are **Kurds** and we are **refugees** from Kirkuk in Iraq. I've lived in Britain for three years. At home, we speak the **Sorani** form of Kurdish and we eat Kurdish food.

That's me wearing red. I'm eating lamb with rice. I also love **dolma**.

Try speaking in Kurdish!

Hello, my name is ...
Choni, min naom ....

What's your name?
Tor nowt thia?

Where are you from?
Khalki chwe? ('kh' as in 'loch')

I'm from Kirkuk.
Min la Kirkuk la dikeboom
('oo' as in 'book')

(Look out for more Kurdish words in this book.)

I love playing outdoors. Today I'm fishing for newts in our friend Jane's garden.

I like dancing with my friends, drawing and playing draughts. I enjoy music too, and I'm learning to play the recorder. I love sport, especially basketball. My favourite TV programme is *Dr Who*.

I play draughts with my brother Bynar. I'm very good!

Meet my family

We live in a flat on a housing estate near the centre of Hull.

I live with my mum, dad and two brothers in Hull in the north of England. My mum is called Amena. She studies English and looks after the family. My dad's name is Ali. He works at a cake factory. He usually has to get up at 4.30 a.m. to arrive on time.

Mum cooks traditional Kurdish food every day. I sometimes help her, and I wash up too.

My brother Byshar is 13, and Bynar is 11. They both like football and play for the Thornton Bashers. I play football too.

Dad used to be a keen footballer and he helps us train.

Mum has a brother in Birmingham. Her nephew (her sister's son) also lives there. The rest of our family, including my two grandparents, still live in northern Iraq.

Bynar says:

"The Thornton Bashers is a new team but we finished third in the league this year. Byshar and I both won medals."

About Iraq

Here is a map of Iraq. My home city of Kirkuk is in the north.

From 1979 to 2003, Saddam Hussein was ruler of Iraq. In 1990 he invaded Kuwait, and the USA led an attack on Iraq to defend Kuwait.

In 2003, US-led forces entered Iraq again and overthrew the government. Since then there has been conflict between the US-led forces and the Iraqis, and between different groups in Iraq.

Dad likes to show me photos of Kirkuk.

The Kurds are one of the groups. Throughout history, they have wanted to rule themselves. When Saddam Hussein was ruler, Kurdish organisations in Iraq fought the government, which used cruel methods to stop them. Many Kurds were killed.

Since the fall of Saddam Hussein, the Kurds have ruled their own community in northern Iraq.

Kurds in Kirkuk with their Kurdish flag. They want Kirkuk to be part of the Kurdish-ruled area they call **Kurdistan.**

Our life in Iraq

In Kirkuk my brothers and I used to play games outside, such as football and hide-and-seek.

Byshar says:

"I remember that we had a really big house, and our grandma lived next door. We used to go in and out of her house all the time."

This photo of me with my dad and Bynar was taken when we all still lived in Kirkuk.

Here I'm in a horse-drawn carriage with my mum and cousins.

My brothers went to school, but I was too young.

My brothers went to primary school in Iraq. School was stricter than it is in England. Pupils sat two to a desk, facing the teacher. All the lessons were in Arabic, the main language in Iraq.

Byshar is watching Kurdish satellite TV. We often watch to keep up with news from Kurdistan and Iraq.

Dad was active in an organisation that fought for the Kurds to rule themselves. It became dangerous for him to stay in Iraq.

13

Moving to Britain

The families of these children are refugees from Iraq. The children come to special classes at the weekend to learn Arabic.

My dad fled Iraq in 2002, when Saddam Hussein was still in power. He went to Hull because he knew other Kurdish people there.

Banoo's dad says:

"I feel safe here. In Iraq, the government treated the Kurds unfairly. Here, I am treated the same as other people."

We joined Dad in October 2004, when I was five. We went to Jordan and then flew to London. Dad came to meet us. Bynar and I didn't recognise him because we hadn't seen him for so long.

I felt really shy at first. The only word I knew in English was 'yes'.

This is the estate where we live. There's a balcony outside the front door but we have no garden to play in.

Dad is walking in the park with Ruth. They met when she was a refugee support worker. Ruth helped Kurdish refugees who arrived in Hull.

My new hometown

Hull is a city by the sea in north-east England with a large **port**. New shops and homes are being built in the city centre, and there is a brand-new sports centre. Rugby is a very popular sport in Hull.

This is a local Kurdish shop. Kurdish refugees have set up a number of shops and restaurants in Hull.

Banoo's mum says:

"There are some problems in Hull. Some people take **drugs** or smash windows, and I hear bad language. A few people make **racist** comments. But generally life is much better for us here."

We came to Hull because Dad was already settled here. I like it because there are more activities for children than there were in Kirkuk. We can go swimming, bowling, to the park or to the zoo.

Hull **marina** is a harbour for small boats, by the river. The area near the river has recently been rebuilt.

We sometimes visit the Deep, a beautiful **aquarium** in the **riverfront** area.

Going to school

Mum takes me to school and picks me up.

I went into Year 2 at Adelaide Primary School and now I'm in Year 5.

My brothers and I found it hard starting school because we didn't speak any English. I had a special teacher called Miss Brook who helped me to learn English. I can read English well now so I can help other children.

During break time, I help Kieran in Year 3 with his reading.

At our school there are children from many different countries. Apart from English, the most common languages the pupils speak are Kurdish, Arabic and **Punjabi**.

Mr McIlwaine told us two players from the rugby club Hull FC are coming to visit. They are judging a competition to design a poster that encourages kids to be healthy.

My school day

Here I'm working on my poster for the competition.

My favourite activity at school is PE. I enjoy rounders, and I play basketball at the sports club. I'm also keen on art, science and maths.

School words

Maths	*Beerkery*
Writing	*Nusin*
Reading	*Khwendenoa*
Pen	*Kalam or Penoos* (`oo' as in wood)
Pencil	*Kalam dar* (dar means wood)
Desk	*Mess*
Chair	*Kursi*
Teacher	*Mamoosta* (`oo' as in wood)

The Hull FC rugby players taught us some rugby skills.

I love reading, especially information books about rabbits, hamsters and other pets. Tracy Beaker and Horrid Henry are my favourite storybooks, and I like fairy stories too.

For lunch, I usually have school dinners. The best meal is fish, chips and beans.

Here I am having school dinner with my best friend Courtney.

At break and lunchtime, I like skipping.

Free time

We spend our free time with both Kurdish and English friends. Our Kurdish friends often come round for a meal. We also like to visit my dad's friend Ruth and her mum Jane.

I'm good friends with Ruth's son Jacob and we play with his guinea pig together.

Bynar, Jacob and I like to help clear Jane's garden.

Ruth says:

"I met Ali when he first came to Britain and now our families are all friends. I take the children to my house or to my mum's so they have a chance to play outside in a big garden."

I go to a school club that organises trips. Sometimes we go to Big Fun, an indoor play centre with scary slides and huge ball pits. I also love going swimming.

Every Saturday, my brothers and I go to a Kurdish centre to learn to read and write our language. We also learn Kurdish songs and dancing.

I can read Kurdish a little now. We get books out of the library, and Mum helps me to read them.

Keeping our culture

We celebrate both Kurdish and Muslim festivals. On 21 March we celebrate Nowroz, the Kurdish New Year. Kurdish people gather outside Hull and build a bonfire. We sing and dance and eat traditional dishes. In Kurdistan, the holiday lasts a week. Here, we celebrate on the closest weekend.

For special occasions, I wear a Kurdish outfit called a kras kurdi. It has a dress, waistcoat and belt.

This is a Kurdish get-together in Manchester. Dad is wearing a traditional brown shalwar – baggy trousers with a top, like a jump suit.

We are Muslims, and we go to the mosque for **Id ul-Fitr** and **Id ul-Adha**. At Id, we wear new clothes and our parents give us money. We eat special dishes, including soup made with apricots, and chicken and rice.

Kurdish foods

Fried meat and rice balls	*Kubbeh* ('u' as in 'book')
Bread	*Nan sarji*
Lamb	*Berkh* ('kh' as in 'ch' in 'loch')
Yogurt	*Maast*
Stuffed vine leaves	*Dolma*
Chick-pea soup	*Nok ow* ('ow' as in 'how')
Rice	*Brinj*
Tea	*Cha*

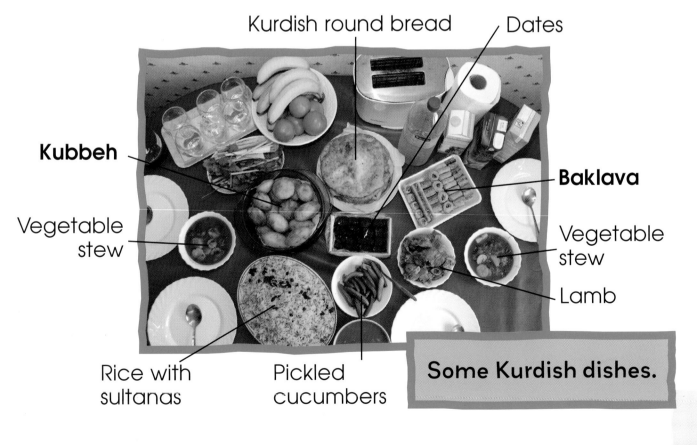

Kurdish round bread   Dates

Kubbeh

Baklava

Vegetable stew

Vegetable stew

Lamb

Rice with sultanas   Pickled cucumbers

Some Kurdish dishes.

My future

Dad says it's not safe to return to Iraq because of the war. If the US and British forces leave, perhaps Iran or Turkey will attack the Kurds in northern Iraq and there will be more conflict.

Banoo's mum says:

"The fighting between different religious groups in Iraq makes me very sad. It's too dangerous to go back. We've made our home in Britain, and the children are settled here."

Bynar, me and Byshar. Byshar is a big Arsenal fan and would like to be a footballer when he grows up.

I am used to living in Britain and would like to stay here. When I grow up, I'd like to go to college. I want to train to be an artist or a designer.

I would love to use my skills in art in my job when I grow up.

I'd also love to learn to play the piano like Ruth.

Ruth is a music teacher. She shows me how to play the piano.

Glossary

aquarium
A place where people can go to see fish and other water animals.

baklava
A rich pastry filled with nuts, honey and sweet spices.

dolma
A dish usually made with leaves from the grapevine stuffed with rice, lamb and onion.

drugs
Illegal substances that some people take, which can be harmful.

Id ul-Adha
The Muslim festival at the end of the pilgrimage to Makkah, celebrated by Muslims all over the world. People eat a feast, visit friends and family and give presents.

Id ul-Fitr
The Muslim festival that marks the end of Ramadan, the Muslim month of fasting.

kubbeh
Balls of minced meat, pine nuts, raisins and spices, covered with rice or grains and deep fried.

Kurdistan
The area where most Kurds live. It stretches across parts of Iran, Iraq and Turkey and small areas of Syria and Armenia.

Kurds
People from a region known as Kurdistan, who have their own culture and language.

marina
A harbour designed for small boats.

port
A place where ships load and unload goods.

Punjabi
The language of the people from the Punjab area in north-west India and Pakistan.

racist
Treating people unfairly because of their skin colour or culture.

refugee
A person who escapes to another country to seek safety from war, natural disaster or bad treatment.

riverfront
The area along a river.

Sorani
The form of the Kurdish language spoken by Kurds in Iran and Iraq. It is written using the Arabic alphabet.

Iraq fact file

Location: The Middle East, with Turkey to the north, Iran to the east, Syria and Jordan to the west, and Saudi Arabia and Kuwait to the south

Climate: Mostly desert, but with more rain in mountainous areas

Capital city: Baghdad

Population: 27 million

Life expectancy at birth (the average age people live to): 69

Main religion: Islam

Language: Arabic. Kurdish is spoken in Kurdistan

Literacy (the percentage of people over 15 who can read and write): 74% (in 2000)

Main jobs: Most people work in industry but many are without jobs because of the war

Number of Iraqi refugees: 2.2 million. Around another 2.2 million Iraqis are internally displaced (they have had to leave their homes but are still in Iraq)

Index

Further information

Websites
http://news.bbc.co.uk/1/hi/
world/middle_east/country_
profiles/791014.stm

Timeline: Iraqi Kurds
http://news.bbc.co.uk/1/hi/
world/middle_east/country_
profiles/2893067.stm

Note to parents and teachers: Please note that these websites are **not** specifically for children and we strongly advise that Internet access is supervised by a responsible adult.